Dedicated to Alyson,

My Inspiration

THE CASE OF THE MISSING DEDICATION TO SCIENCE

THE CASE OF THE MOST FUN FIRST YEAR DORM EXPERIENCE EVER

THE CASE OF THE MISSING DEDICATION TO SERVICE

THE CASE OF A FAITH BASED MOTIVATION FOR MEDICINE

THE CASE OF THE VERY INVOLVED PARENT

THE CASE OF THE RECOVERING ALCOHOLIC APPLICANT

THE CASE OF THE APPLICANT WITH AN EPIPHANY BASED MOTIVATION

THE CASE OF THE APPLICANT WITH A MISSING DEDICATION TO EXCELLENCE

THE CASE OF THE REJECTED APPLICANT WITH "PERFECT NUMBERS"

THE CASE OF THE WELL-KNOWN APPLICANT

THE CASE OF THE APPLICANT WITH A LONG DISTANCE TRAVELED

SUMMARY OF LESSONS LEARNED

SUMMARY OF QUESTIONS TO GUIDE APPLICANTS

ACKNOWLEDGMENTS

Case Studies in Medical School Admissions

I have resisted putting these words to paper. How can I, as someone who has seen and advocated for the power of individual advising, provide helpful general advice? Now, after returning to full time advising, I have reflected on the many applicants I have been privileged to know over my 30 years in advising and admissions and hope that by reviewing lessons I have learned you may find them to be useful whether you are an applicant, an advisor or a medical school admissions committee member.

As you begin, it may be helpful for you to understand my background, experiences, and career path. The example of a life dedicated to service was provided by my formative role models. My initial exploration of a career in computer science provided a foundation for an understanding of, enthusiasm for, and ability to participate in technological advancements which I continue to find helpful. On my way to my computer science classes each day however, I walked by the campus Speech and Hearing Clinic. The activities around that building intrigued me and, after my first course in language development, I understood I had found a path I needed to explore. I thrived in the science requirements and the clinical preparation. I eagerly explored opportunities in nursing homes, hospitals, and schools. And, then, I committed to working as a Speech and Language Pathologist in a state prison system. This experience was transformative in many ways. I learned about my abilities to relate my training to novel environments and requirements. I developed an in-depth understanding of the realities of the disparities in our educational and health care systems. I learned there are children born into circumstances with little opportunity for understanding hope. I developed great respect for them. My decision to explore these realities and what they meant to my prior understanding of the world took to me to seminary and

Hyde Park. It was there, through one opportunity and then another, I began my work in premedical advising. While my family and I served as dormitory resident heads, I began working as a general advisor, then the Chief Health Professions Advisor, and finally, as the Assistant Dean for Admissions and Financial Aid at the University of Chicago Pritzker School of Medicine. I will always be grateful for the opportunities that have led me to put these words to paper.

Each of the included cases is based on my experiences. The identifying details of individuals and institutions have been changed to protect their identity.

I hope you find these words to be useful. Please know, I also add my best wishes in the important work you are doing

THE CASE OF THE MISSING DEDICATION TO SCIENCE

BACKGROUND

Lily grew up in a loving and caring home where both parents were strong role models as hard-working professionals, both dedicated to community service. Lily began her own community volunteering during her middle school years and soon after decided she wanted to be a doctor. By the time of her high school graduation she was leading groups of her peers in several important community initiatives. On any given week she could be found at the local food bank helping visitors select groceries, reading with hospitalized children at the area hospital, playing music at nearby nursing homes, and coaching a child with a physical disability in a soccer program. And, Lily found great joy in her participation in the local community theater as a performer as well as an energetic backstage contributor.

COLLEGE YEARS

Based on her very successful high school experience Lily was accepted at each college to which she applied. She chose to attend a highly selective liberal arts college and quickly moved back into her high school role as a leader and an effective volunteer in a wide range of efforts. She also immediately joined in the opportunities available to continue her passion for performing and music.

Lily was very pleased to learn she could use her AP credit to replace her college's math requirement. And, she was thrilled to learn that most medical schools would accept her AP General Chemistry to fulfill that requirement. After some exploration, she decided to fulfill the premedical requirements while majoring in History along with a minor in Public Policy. In her first two quarters, she took general education requirements and introductory History courses. She easily excelled. In her third quarter she took a History Course, a Psychology course, a Statistics course, and an introductory Biology course. For the first time in Lily's experience in her science and math classes she received a B and a B- while achieving As in the others. While she was shaken by this, she was very busy and decided she had just not put enough time into her coursework and that she could easily fix that in the coming year.

With the beginning of her second year Lily moved into a few leadership roles in her activities and continued to participate in all of them. Her level of energy and enthusiasm for service made her a well-known and well-respected student, both by her peers and her faculty. In meeting with her premedical advisor, they laid out a plan for her to apply at the end of her fourth year of college so that she would only need to take, at the most, one science class at a time.

By the time of her graduation Lily had been able to earn honors in both History and Public Policy, having completed a thesis which integrated a question she was passionate about which crossed these two disciplines. She also earned awards for her important contributions in service and campus leadership. For her medical school application, the Dean of Students wrote an outstanding letter of recommendation on her behalf and her History advisor spoke with enthusiasm about her potential for scholarship. She was able to obtain a strong letter from her organic chemistry professor who stressed that Lily's Bs throughout the 2-quarter course were impacted by the commitments she had in other classes and extracurricular responsibilities. Her second science letter would have to be described as generic. She hoped to be able to also receive a letter from the principal of the high school where she would teach history during the upcoming year.

Lily's strong test taking abilities allowed her to achieve an above average MCAT score with little time devoted to study. Her overall grade point average was outstanding in the non-sciences and average in the sciences. She worked closely with her premedical advisor and gave careful attention to each component of the application process. By the summer after her graduation, she had achieved four medical school interviews. She enjoyed this part of the process and left a positive impression at each medical school she visited.

MEDICAL SCHOOL YEARS

After being accepted at three of her four schools of interview, Lily chose to attend a mid-tier private medical school. She was drawn to the small class size, the community service focus, and a small scholarship that would help reduce the financial burden. She understood she would graduate with $200,000+ debt.

By the end of orientation Lily was identified by peers and faculty as someone who would be a leader in community service and Dean's Council activities. By the time classes began, she was very busy with extracurricular activities and had made connections with almost everyone in her class. As classes began, she was surprised by how much time her classmates were devoting to study. While she was a responsible student, she found herself much more excited about time spent in extracurriculars. And, for the first time in her life, Lily did not find herself excelling as a student. As she achieved below average results in her coursework, she spent more time in extracurriculars where she did find success and positive feedback. As the first year continued, she found herself less and less interested in her coursework and found it difficult to study. By the end of the year, when she met with her advisor, Lily did not know if she could continue. She described herself as a failure and did not indicate the strategies needed to get on track academically. She was unable to identify a time she had failed in the past.

Lily did graduate from medical school, but it was not with honors and it was not an experience she looks back on with positive feelings. She had to give up her leadership activities and most of her community service so that she could be successful academically. She tried to continue her music and performance interests, but eventually left those behind as she was not able to achieve the level of excellence in them which she found acceptable. While Lily's performance in the clinical years was stronger than in the preclinical years, her frustration only grew with the expectation in terms of science knowledge even in the clinical years.

OUTCOMES

A pediatric residency close to home seemed to bring a sigh of relief for Lily. Finally, she thought she could do what she always wanted to do, take care of patients. During the residency however, Lily found her weak science foundation and lack of time to participate in outside activities to be a frustration. She left after sixteen months. She and her family developed a plan to address her $200,000+ debt as she sought the education credentials needed to teach high school history. After a few years of teaching and a return to community service, Lily decided to pursue a History graduate degree.

LESSONS LEARNED

*A passion for learning across disciplines, with a particular interest in the sciences is required as a part of an appropriate motivation for, and success in, a career in medicine.

*Experience with a combination of rigorous science classes at one time is important in evaluating potential for success in the medical school curriculum.

*Evidence of resilience is required to suggest readiness for medical school.

*Admissions committees can be blinded by extraordinary extracurricular leadership and interpersonal skills. Don't be.

*Decisions made to become a physician early in life must be reexamined carefully with mature reflection on how interests and strengths have developed.

QUESTIONS TO GUIDE APPLICANTS

*Are you energized by your science classes and find yourself able to excel in those academic terms when you take more than one science class?

*Will you be eager to be a life-long learner, particularly in the sciences?

*Have you learned how to "bounce" back, to do something that requires hard work and persistence. Have you developed resilience?

*Have you learned to accept less than perfection from yourself in some of your efforts? Are you able to contribute in situations where you are not the "star"?

*If you made your decision to become a physician at a young age, have you honestly reexamined your motivation as you have matured?

The Case of the Most Fun First Year Dorm Experience Ever

BACKGROUND

As the oldest of six children, Andrew learned to take responsibility from a young age. His parents had demanding jobs, with his father working two jobs to help make ends meet. The welfare and education of the children was always the priority for the family with study time being a part of each evening's expectation. Although his parents did not have experience in the college application process, they encouraged Andrew to take advantage of the resources in his high school. He did that and his outstanding high school academics and extracurricular leadership combined with thoughtful and sincere essays led him to 5 college acceptances, each offering significant need-based scholarships. While he found it difficult to move far from family, he chose the school that offered the biggest scholarship and would allow him to explore his many career interests, even though it meant only returning home for holidays.

COLLEGE YEARS

Everything about college was new. Andrew no longer had an alarm set so he could help his younger siblings with breakfast and getting to school. His family chores and extracurriculars no longer helped provide structure for his day. And, he was fascinated by learning everything he could from the people he was meeting from such very different backgrounds. He spent hours in the dorm lounge at night talking to other residents. He was thrilled when he was invited to a party and soon after found himself spending more and more of his time in what was known as the dorm's "party suite" where there was always someone available to talk and also some alcohol to be shared. Andrew was able to achieve an average performance in his classes without much effort, studying only evenings before an exam.

By the end of the second quarter, Andrew and his friends had received three disciplinary warnings for noise and alcohol violations. When they were argumentative with the Resident Heads during a "finals week party", they were moved to single rooms in separate dorms around campus and placed on disciplinary probation until the time of their graduation. This proved to be a "wake up call" for Andrew as he went home and had to explain his new address and average grades to his parents. He returned for the final quarter of his freshman year determined to get himself on track.

Upon his return, Andrew met with his new Resident Heads who helped him identify resources to explore. He chose to join a student organization dedicated to working with children at an area homeless shelter for women and children. He met several times with a counselor to discuss the impact of alcohol use on the choices he had made. He also began meeting regularly with his academic advisor. At the end of the school year, Andrew was excelling in his coursework, selected for leadership in the service group for the following year, and a positive member of his dormitory community.

Over the summer, Andrew returned home and worked on two different construction crews to help fund his college expenses and also help his family. He was called home urgently one day as his youngest sister had experienced a serious head injury. Over the next few weeks, Andrew spent his days at the construction sites and his evenings at his sister's hospital bedside. During those two weeks,

Andrew's eyes were opened to the work of physicians and the needs of pediatric patients.

When he returned to school in the fall, he met with the premedical advisor and tentatively asked for help in exploring his growing interest in medicine. Would his disciplinary record make this impossible? Together, they made a plan so that the advisor could come to know Andrew well while Andrew could continue to explore his interests in medicine and could demonstrate the level of integrity, responsibility, and maturity needed to succeed in medical school and in the future as a professional. When he was selected to be a Resident Assistant for his senior year, the advisor felt Andrew was ready to answer the concerns of admissions committees and he began the application process at the end of his Senior year. He gave careful attention to each aspect of the application process. In writing about the institutional actions, he took full responsibility for his behavior and made clear the lessons he had learned. He received outstanding letters of recommendation from faculty and the Dean of Student's Office. For his application year he took a position as a scribe in a pediatric clinic and would later receive an exceptional letter from the physicians in that practice.

Andrew applied broadly and was thrilled to be accepted to a state school close to his home.

MEDICAL SCHOOL YEARS
While Andrew found many new challenges as he began medical school, he was ready this time. He took advantage of faculty and peer advising resources and soon became a sought-after member for any study group. His maturity and level of responsibility made him a leader when conflicts arose in the class. Faculty and administration regularly sought his participation as a student representative on their committees.

OUTCOMES

From the beginning of medical school, Andrew had excelled in clinical experiences. He pursued his interest in pediatrics and ultimately entered a residency in pediatrics. A fellowship in pediatric oncology followed the completion of his residency and he is now a beloved practicing physician back in his home community.

LESSONS LEARNED

*Institutional actions should not be disqualifying, but evidence is required to demonstrate the needed level of responsibility, maturity, and integrity.

*Strong letters of recommendation from those who know the applicant well are always important, but particularly so in cases where institutional actions are an issue.

*Evidence of the strategies needed for making successful transitions are important to consider in the medical school admissions process.

*It is important to respect the journeys and diverse perspective and experiences of applicants who are first generation college students.

QUESTIONS TO GUIDE APPLICANTS

*There is no one right path to college and medical school. Find the path right for you and begin college or medical school only when you are ready to excel in all areas of your life. Sometimes this will require taking time in between graduation and matriculation. What can you do during this time to strengthen your readiness?

*If you had a difficult transition to college, what have you learned that insures your transition to medical will be successful?

*Are you able to obtain letters of recommendation which speak to your maturity, integrity, motivation and intellectual and personal readiness to be an outstanding medical student?

*How will you develop a support system in medical school that allows you to learn with and from those with similar values and goals?

The Case of the Missing Dedication to Service

Background

Jennifer grew up surrounded by people dedicated to addressing her needs and supporting her efforts. Her parents were both very busy physicians and spared no expense in ensuring she and her siblings would be able to take advantage of every available resource. In high school, Jennifer chose an elite boarding school and excelled there academically. School breaks were spent traveling with friends or attending language immersion and test prep boot camps. The school's guidance counselor suggested she give herself a competitive advantage in the application process by doing a gap year before college. She was pleased to follow this advice and spent the year in an internship pursuing basic science research. She worked responsibly and enjoyed the science she learned. She did not excel, however. She found it difficult to adjust to living independently and struggled to organize her food and laundry needs since these had always been provided.

When it was time to submit her college applications, Jennifer struggled with essays about her values and a vision for her future. She had followed the counselor's advice about the gap year, but had not followed the advice to engage in community service activities, explaining that all she could find was "grunt work" opportunities. Based on outstanding academics and test scores, and solid letters of recommendation, she was accepted to four strong schools, a small liberal arts college, a mid-sized university, and two state schools in her home state. She chose the small liberal arts college and was eager to get back to school.

COLLEGE YEARS

Returning to dormitory life was in many ways a relief in terms of the resources available to help with daily living. Jennifer volunteered for the University Food Services committee to give input regarding her concerns about the quality of the food and lack of flexibility of hours. Other residents saw her as someone who had adjusted to dormitory living in the past and nominated her for House Council. She declined the nomination explaining she would not be available for the Sunday evening required meetings because it was an important study night for her.

Jennifer joined a sorority as soon as it was allowed. She was a positive and energetic member and did participate in the required service activities. None of them interested her enough however to continue to participate beyond the minimum required.

After excelling in the general education requirements, the end of the second year brought the need for Jennifer to declare a major. She did not find herself passionate about any subject, but did enjoy the sciences more than the writing and discussion classes, particularly those where she needed to work in small groups to achieve a goal. She declared a biology major and her advisor encouraged her to begin to focus on what she hoped to pursue after graduation and throughout her life. After talking with her parents and attending information sessions about PhD opportunities, she decided to become a physician.

Jennifer's premedical advisor discussed the expected and needed competencies for entering medical school students and pointed out the areas for needed improvement before she could apply successfully. Once again, Jennifer was advised to become involved in community service activities as well as clinical opportunities. She explained that her parents were both physicians, so she knew all about medicine and that her parents did not think it is worth her time to "mop floors in an ER" or "do grunt work" at a clinic. She did share that her parents were arranging shadowing opportunities for her over upcoming school breaks.

The medical school application process was a difficult one for Jennifer. While her letter writers saw her as a personable and energetic student, they could not speak to her motivation for medicine. She herself found it difficult to answer questions about her motivation, how she would contribute to diversity, and how she could be an advocate for others. Her applications were submitted late in the process. She left each of her medical school interviews frustrated by the questions which focused on her motivation for medicine. She was accepted off waitlists at the two schools her parents had attended and chose the one with the higher "ranking". She and her parents were disappointed by these results. Her parents lodged complaints about the premedical advising process to the advisor and the President's Office.

MEDICAL SCHOOL YEARS

The transition to medical school was not easy for Jennifer. She found herself frustrated by the expectations for participation in small groups for most of the curriculum requirements. In talking with her advising dean about this, Jennifer explained that other students were slower and less capable and the whole experience was a waste of time. And, she found it difficult to understand that her schedule was no longer in her control. A friend's wedding, for example, came at a time when there were activities with required attendance. While her request to be away during this time was denied, she was able to arrive the night before the wedding where she spent the time complaining about her unreasonable medical school dean.

This frustration and increasing anger worsened during the clinical years. Feedback from peer evaluations described her as someone who was eager to have others do her work and as someone who took every opportunity to leave early and arrive late. They also described her as harsh in her interactions with patients and their families. This behavior was also seen in her interactions with nurses. Several incident reports were filed which described Jennifer's lack of interest in patient interaction and attempts to have the nurses understand that this was their job.

Jennifer's Dean of Students reached out to her regularly during the third year. In their conversations, the Dean encouraged Jennifer to become more engaged with her classmates and to spend time in the free clinic setting where she could come to understand the importance of working with the entire health care team. The Dean also talked with her about her future goals. Jennifer was not open to the advice to explore her interests and was not able to hear the concerns expressed by the Dean. She was convinced that medical school policies and her classmates were the problems. Her parents supported this view, and as she complained to her parents, they regularly shared their displeasure with the Dean. Jennifer was confident that once she finished medical school, could control her schedule, and hire her own nurses that she would enjoy being a doctor.

OUTCOMES

Finishing around the middle of her class Jennifer struggled in the residency match process. She was able to obtain a position in Internal Medicine at a hospital close to home. She once again breathed a sigh of relief as she returned home and the resources available there. She did finish the residency and took a position in a practice of one of her parents' colleagues. After working for two years, she married and left her position. Three years later, she has no intention of returning to practice in any capacity.

Lessons Learned

*A history of, enthusiasm for, sustained participation in service, and clinical activities are important in predicting success in medical school.

*Applicants will sometimes hear advice from those who are ill informed about current standards and expectations for medical school admissions. It is important to give applicants opportunities to hear informed advice from resources they can be encouraged to trust.

*Advisors face very complicated demands and sometimes competing roles. Their constituents include the applicant, the applicant's parents, the institution's enrollment goals, the faculty who support the premedical curriculum, the medical schools, and the applicant's future patients. It is important advisors receive full support for their work from their institutions.

*While family, supporters, development officers, and schools may think they are being helpful in paving the way for admission for applicants, this seldom leads to a positive outcome. The best processes have firewalls to prevent this influence from impacting admissions decisions.

Questions to Guide Applicants

*Are you passionate about using your life in service to others, putting the needs of others before your own?

*Are you eager to work together with a team to achieve a common goal?

*Have you learned to live as an independent adult, taking care of your needs in all areas of your life while also supporting those around you?

*Do you respect the experience and advice of others?

*If you could anything you could dream of in the coming year what would it be? Does it embody the values of learning and service

THE CASE OF A FAITH BASED MOTIVATION FOR MEDICINE

BACKGROUND

Jonah was raised in an intergenerational family home with strong ties and commitment to their church and religious tradition. The neighborhood in which he was born and raised was one where the great majority of families were involved in one of the faith communities which dotted almost every corner. Sunday's were spent in Sunday School and services. Wednesday evenings were devoted to age group church Bible Studies. Fridays were service nights with church members assigned to participate in activities ranging from hospital visitation to food pantry stocking. Jonah eagerly participated in all activities and as he became a teenager, he took on leadership roles. He sought out additional service activities in which he could participate during school breaks. He found himself particularly drawn to activities that allowed him to spend time with elderly populations.

Jonah excelled in all of his high school coursework and in doing so developed strong study habits and organization skills. Faculty and peers had great respect for him as a person of integrity and service. His circle of friends was small, but did include students both inside and outside of his church community. Basically, he was a student all parents hoped their children would spend time with. Jonah developed a particularly strong relationship with a teacher from a faith tradition different from his own. They had regular conversations in which they shared their beliefs and Jonah developed an eagerness to hear of the faith traditions and experiences of others.

All aspects of the college application process went smoothly for Jonah. His outstanding grades and test scores combined with significant service and leadership experiences and exceptionally strong letters of recommendation. He applied to large universities and small colleges close to home. One of his priorities for choosing a school was the strength of its resources for him to continue to participate in a faith-based community. He chose a large university and eagerly looked forward to beginning college in a place where he could also regularly return home to his family and church.

College Years

His maturity and the clarity of his values made the transition to college an easy one for Jonah. He was respected in his dorm and regularly sought after for advice. His quiet and steady leadership style made him a natural choice for positions of responsibility in dorm life. And, as his faculty grew to know him, he was regularly identified as a student who could contribute very effectively in advisory committees. Jonah did make his university faith community a priority in organizing his activities and gradually took leadership in interfaith dialogue events.

Several of Jonah's faculty spoke to him individually about his career interests and encouraged him to pursue advanced study in their disciplines. Jonah appreciated their input and spoke regularly with his college advisor about how to choose a career path. He also spoke with his home pastor about his thinking and he described finding clarity and peace from these discussions.

Service activities were a part of Jonah's college life from the beginning. He again was drawn to activities that included care for the elderly. In thinking about his future, he decided he wanted a career which focused on service and care of others. Because of his love for the sciences, he began to seriously consider medicine as an option. He made an appointment to meet with a premedical advisor and met with two physicians from his home church over a school break.

As he entered his sophomore year of college and began learning more about the work of the physician, Jonah's decision for medicine grew in its strength and clarity. He felt he had found his calling and that medicine was the path for him to make his most meaningful contributions. Faculty and advisors were enthusiastic in encouraging him in this path. He continued to excel in his coursework, took leadership on campus in faith-based organizations, eagerly began work in a research lab which led to a very successful senior project, and worked closely with the premedical advisor to learn about the application process.

Jonah prepared all components of the process with sincerity and openness. He spoke of the importance of his faith in giving him the clarity of motivation, the strength to care for others, and the resilience needed for the challenges ahead. His advisor worked with him to make certain he indicated his respect for the beliefs of others in writing about the role of his religious beliefs. Each of his letter writers read his personal statement in advance of their interview. One faculty member challenged Jonah, saying that it was impossible to be a person of science and also a person of faith. Jonah responded with respect for the views of the faculty member and outlined the way in which he reconciles these issues for himself.

Jonah's attention to the process led to a very successful outcome. He received his first of eight interviews in mid-July and had several acceptances delivered on October 15. His decision again prioritized the ability to remain involved in his faith- based community and he was intentional about asking to speak with involved faculty during his revisit weekend experiences. He ultimately chose a medical school with a strong service outreach to elderly populations in the setting of a university with resources to continue his inter-faith dialogue leadership.

Jonah's advisor reached out for feedback to several medical schools where she expected Jonah would have been accepted. She was told that some reviewers were concerned about the role of faith in his life and that he might be a proselytizing presence with patients and peers.

MEDICAL SCHOOL YEARS

Jonah excelled in all aspects of the medical school curriculum. He continued his commitment to service and became a leader in several Dean's advisory group efforts. His calm, mature, and professional presence led him to become a beloved peer and colleague. Each morning, as early arriving staff entered their offices, they greeted Jonah in the student lounge as he quietly read his Bible. Some mornings other students joined him, but Jonah was always there.

In clinical settings, Jonah brought a calm and confidence to his interactions with patients. He was a role model to others in the ways in which he demonstrated culturally competent care.

OUTCOMES

The residency process brought more success for Jonah, success he accepted with grace and gratitude. He moved across the country to join a residency program in Internal Medicine and later did a fellowship in Geriatrics. He chose this program because of the opportunity to join a faculty member's research in Religion and Medicine. Jonah is now back close to home and a beloved member of his community and church. His quiet leadership continues to be an inspiration to many. His dedication to mentorship finds him regularly meeting with aspiring premedical students who are asking questions about their faith and science.

LESSONS LEARNED

*It is important that the medical school interview process allow for the identification of the quiet and steady leaders who are often overlooked in the face of more extroverted applicants.

*Applicants will find the best fit in their medical school search by identifying their priorities and the strength of the resources available on each campus to pursue these.

*It is very helpful for college faculty who are familiar with medical school admissions expectations to make themselves available for interviews with applicants, using the personal statement and activities as material for their questions.

*In discussing the role of faith in one's motivation for medicine, it is important to make clear a dedication to respect and celebrate the religious beliefs and traditions of all others.

*College faculty, premedical advisors, and admissions committees should examine the biases they hold regarding issues of religion and the practice of medicine.

QUESTIONS TO GUIDE APPLICANTS

*Have you sought advice about your career interests from trusted mentors, in several areas of your life, who have come to know you well?

*What resources are important to you as you live a life which is true to the values which shape and sustain you?

*Are you dedicated to growing as a culturally competent person and future physician?

*Why is a career as a physician the best way for you to achieve your life's goals?

The Case of the Very Involved Parent

Background

There had been family and educational challenges in Nathan's developmental years, and at each turn, his parents had been very involved in finding solutions and leading decision making. As the youngest of three children by more than ten years, and the only son, his mother, at his father's direction, had ample time to devote to being certain the path ahead was as smooth as possible. Her passion for his success grew alongside her pride in his success.

The local schools did not have the resources which easily led many of their graduates to attend the elite colleges that Nathan's mother wanted him to have as choices. This led her to find additional resources for Nathan's participation. While he found himself too busy to complete the many applications for enrichment opportunities, his mother was happy to do this on his behalf and Nathan was happy to attend the science and sports camps his mother identified. Nathan was also busy during his high school years with his commitment to community service, having as his mother described, "a big heart to help those in need".

When high school graduation arrived, he followed his parents' advice to strengthen his college application by taking a year in a study abroad program before college matriculation. Since he was very busy throughout the year with this program, they continued the pattern where his mother wrote and submitted the bulk of his college essays. In the end, there were several acceptances at elite schools and Nathan chose to attend the strongest school that would allow him to best pursue his growing interest in science and service.

COLLEGE YEARS

The transition to college was not smooth for Nathan. His mother's advice was to challenge himself with a rigorous curriculum since he had always excelled in school and needed to continue to "set himself apart". Nathan did hear his advisor's cautions about the relative weaknesses in his high school preparation, but felt strongly that his mother best knew his ability and readiness. The end of the first term saw him with several Cs in general education classes and a B in a science class, a premedical requirement. On reflection, he and his mother decided he needed to spend more time focused on his academics and developed a priority list of the many extracurriculars he had been exploring. He stepped back and developed a plan for the coming term which would hopefully allow for greater academic success. In terms of extracurriculars, he continued his participation in a local homeless shelter and IM sports.

Nathan's confidence was shaken by his difficult move to college and his response was to lean more heavily on his mother for help in editing his written work and basic research for everything from paper development to options for campus jobs. His mother was eager to help and as they saw his academics improve their pattern of working together continued.

During the first term there were several frantic communications between Nathan's mother, his advisor, and the Dean of Students. His mother wanted to be certain they understood Nathan's educational background and his many exceptional qualities. Both the advisor and Dean of Students worked to help her understand they were available as resources, but that the communication needed to be between them and Nathan. She assured them and Nathan did provide in writing that she had permission to speak to them on his behalf.

As Nathan's interest in science continued to grow, he sought research opportunities and found he was able to excel in this environment. He was encouraged to continue pursuing graduate work in the sciences and explored this option. His interactions with the medical director at the homeless shelter where he volunteered did lead him to consider medical school. His mother was very excited about this option and saw it as the perfect fit for Nathan's many strengths and interests. They began to explore the medical school application requirements and based on Nathan's strong interest in research, decided that it would be best to apply to Medical Scientist Training Programs.

The premedical advising program at Nathan's school was very strong and offered many resources for exploration and information about careers in the health professions. Nathan was generally too busy to attend the sessions, but since they were recorded, he was able to give his mother access to the link to watch them. She did this diligently and kept him updated on the timelines and requirements. Nathan met with the premedical advisor, but did not find it to be a satisfying meeting. The advisor stressed that Nathan's grades and MCAT were borderline for success in the MSTP application process and that he needed to pursue more research experience. He reported to his mother who then began reaching out to the premedical advisor to be certain she understood Nathan's many strengths and readiness. The premedical advisor made it clear that she was available to assist Nathan, but that she would not communicate further with his parent.

Senior year brought many responsibilities and as spring graduation events took more and more time, Nathan and his mother decided he would spend a year doing full-time research. With the resources of his school, it was easy for Nathan to find a position and he settled into a lab where he excelled. As spring again arrived, Nathan felt he did not have the time to prepare the medical school applications, so his mother stepped in and provided essays for him to review and approve. They were able to submit the applications for

MST programs and had secondaries completed and returned by the middle of September.

Nathan chose not to make use of his college premedical advising committee letter throughout the process. He instead submitted individual letters of recommendation which he felt would better reflect his strengths and abilities. These included letters from his former and current PI, as well as from his high school principal.

THE MEDICAL SCHOOL APPLICATION

While most of the MST programs were impressed with Nathan's research experience, they found his average grades and MCAT to be of concern. Throughout his secondary responses, he focused his responses to challenge questions on the difficulty he had in transitioning to college because of the weaknesses of his high school education and the lack of support from his college advisor. This attitude raised concern for several medical school committees as well. He did receive two interviews and he and his mother worked to prepare for the possible questions.

In the meantime, Nathan's mother reached out to each of the schools where Nathan had not received an interview. The admissions offices did not take her phone calls and her emails were responded to with a standard message that they would not communicate with anyone other than the applicant. She pushed back on this with permission from Nathan to allow her to speak on his behalf. One school's Dean of Admissions did agree to speak with her.

The Dean listened to the mother and through her tears heard her concern that after working so hard, her son had only received interviews at "second rate schools". The Dean shared that an acceptance to any medical school and/or MST program would be a great opportunity Nathan should eagerly accept. The following day, the Dean received a phone call from Nathan's father. The father explained that his wife was near a nervous breakdown and his family was experiencing a time of great stress. The father asked what he could do for Nathan to be able to have an interview either this year or the next. The Dean explained he understood the stress involved in the process. He outlined how unusual it was for parents to be this involved and perhaps this is something the family should discuss with a trusted resource. And then, the Dean explained that Nathan would not be invited for interview this year. And, that if he were to receive an acceptance to another medical school, the Dean stressed that Nathan should accept it and begin his medical education. He explained that turning down a medical school offer to attend a "better school" would raise significant red flags in a reapplication.

The parents again contacted the Dean when Nathan did receive a MSTP offer from his home state school. The Dean strongly encouraged them to have Nathan consult with his college premedical advising and strongly discouraged their plan to have him decline this MSTP offer and prepare for a reapplication. Nathan did follow the advice of his parents, declined the offer, and reapplied in the next year. This required a retake of the MCAT since his scores had expired at most schools. When learning this would be necessary his mother again contacted the schools and asked for a waiver of this requirement. Nathan ultimately decided to reapply with the previous MCAT to "see what would happen".

OUTCOMES

When Nathan was not accepted to any MST program or MD program, he applied to graduate programs in the Biological Sciences and is now happily well into his PhD program. Nathan completed the graduate applications independently of his mother's advice and assistance.

LESSONS LEARNED

*There are often signs during the admissions process that suggest an applicant's parents are overly involved. In these situations, the applicant's maturity, independence, and readiness should be given additional evaluation.

*In reviewing who has submitted letters of recommendation on behalf of the applicant, it is important to consider those that are submitted, as well as, those that are not chosen for submission.

*The decision to decline a medical school acceptance offer with hopes to reapply and gain an offer at a school perceived as stronger should be seen as a major concern in terms of the applicant's motivation and priorities.

*Applicants enter the medical school application process with a great variance in terms of their maturity and readiness. Admissions Committees should be aware that in some cases, substantial help may have been provided.

QUESTIONS TO GUIDE APPLICANTS

*Are you ready to complete the application to medical school without significant guidance, input, and contribution from your parents?

*How is your decision to pursue medicine influenced and directed by family expectations?

*Are you able to identify and accept feedback from appropriate and knowledgeable resources to guide you in your professional decision making?

*Does your decision to become a physician see prestige as a primary motivation?

THE CASE OF THE RECOVERING ALCOHOLIC APPLICANT

BACKGROUND

A tragedy as a young child drastically changed Anna's life. When her parents were killed in a plane crash Anna was 8 years old. Her three significantly older sisters were already settled in their boarding schools or colleges. After a difficult court battle, Anna's custody was given to a beloved aunt. She was very busy with her life as a physician, but eager to welcome Anna into her home and life.

Anna was a personable and very bright child who quickly adapted to her new environment. She excelled in elementary and middle school and was open to following her aunt's advice that she attend a boarding school for high school. She made the transition with apparent ease and became a leader among her peers in the classroom and community. Her faculty and advisors were drawn to her positive spirit and ability to care for others, particularly her peers in distress.

Anna had many invitations for holiday breaks, so she seldom returned to her aunt's house. During these times, she found that she enjoyed the escape she found from drinking alcohol and it was certainly easily available in many of the homes she visited. At first, she did not continue to drink as she returned to school, but over time, she found herself drinking regularly. When faculty and advisors began to notice a decline in her performance and change in her attitude, Anna was honest with them about her struggle. After evaluation, she agreed to enter a rehabilitation program and delayed her high school graduation by a year.

As she returned to her high school, Anna found a supportive environment and her aunt was now engaged in conversations about Anna's future. With strong letters of recommendation from faculty and the Dean of Students, along with a letter from her physician, Anna was accepted at a number of colleges. She chose a small liberal arts college close to her Aunt's home.

COLLEGE YEARS

The breadth of the coursework available as she entered college energized Anna. She loved learning and loved her community of peers and faculty. During her rehabilitation program, she had begun to think of her career interests. As she found herself passionate about the sciences, she began to more seriously consider a career as a physician. She regularly met with her premedical advisor, shadowed her Aunt in her practice, and began volunteering in a local free clinic and community hospital. She was disciplined about attending daily AA meetings and was focused on staying healthy. She would openly share that this was not easy to achieve. Rather than personable and outgoing as she had been described in high school, faculty and peers now described her as kind, focused, and determined.

Anna applied to medical school with outstanding "numbers", outstanding letters of recommendation, and experiences which made it clear that her motivation was based on a mature and well-explored motivation. She did have two institutional actions on her AMCAS application, one for a noise violation during a freshman year party in her suite and the other, for having alcohol in her possession during a sporting event. Her college premedical advisory committee provided a letter on her behalf in which, with Anna's knowledge, they reviewed her experience as a recovering alcoholic, discussed the institutional actions, and discussed ways in which Anna had been an important resource to her peers struggling with substance abuse. They also recommended her with complete confidence in terms of her readiness, academically and personally, for the rigors of medical school.

After receiving only two interviews, Anna's premedical advisor, with Anna's approval, reached out to several medical schools' Deans for Admissions for advice and to personally express his confidence in Anna's readiness. These calls did result in one additional interview.

Anna reported that all of her interviews had focused on the institutional actions and her experience as a recovering alcoholic. On several interview days, she spent more time in the interviews than the other applicants that day. She felt she had answered all the questions openly and honestly, but left each interview day feeling she would not likely be accepted.

Anna was ultimately accepted at one highly ranked medical school and was humbled and enthusiastic about the opportunity.

MEDICAL SCHOOL YEARS

During the Revisit weekend, Anna was encouraged to make an appointment to meet with the Dean of Admissions. She did this with some hesitation, but in their meeting quickly realized what a wonderful and supportive resource this faculty member would be for her. The Dean explained to Anna that he wanted to encourage her to reach out immediately to the Dean of Student Wellness and that he would be able to facilitate an introduction. The Dean of Admissions stressed he felt this faculty member would be an important resource as Anna approached the many transitions medical school would require. He also stressed the Admissions Committee enthusiasm for her potential in medicine and welcomed her to their community.

Anna did make an appointment to meet with the Dean of Student Wellness and was open with her about her history. The Dean gave Anna information for several AA groups which met daily on campus and they agreed Anna would make this a priority in her life. The Dean asked Anna to contact her immediately if her medical school schedule was making it impossible for her to regularly attend meetings.

Medical school was certainly full of many transitions, but Anna's enthusiasm for all she was learning and her passion for the service opportunities she was engaged in energized her. She was very successful and graduated being named to the Alpha Omega Alpha Honor Medical Society. She applied to residencies in Internal Medicine and matched into her first-choice program. She and her significant other were thrilled they had matched in the same hospital and would be able to begin their careers together.

OUTCOMES

Anna thrived in residency and credited this partly to her dedication to continuing in her AA involvement. She and her now husband, both received outstanding opportunities after their residences and began their professional lives with confidence and enthusiasm. After two years of practice, Anna suffered a relapse and eventually did enter a rehabilitation program for impaired physicians. She was determined to return to the work she loved and has been able to do this successfully. She is open with her practice partners and practice leadership and continues to have the full support of her husband and AA sponsor. She is able to talk openly about the stresses she found in her early years of practice that she was not able to put into perspective on her own. She now returns to her medical school each year and speaks to the entering class about substance abuse and a career in medicine. She also works with the Dean of Student Wellness to meet with any student who asks for an individual appointment with her.

LESSONS LEARNED
*Tragedy and hardship can lead to the resilience and determination needed for success as a medical school student and physician. It should not however be seen as a reason to overlook or explain away any aspect of the applicant's record.

*It is very helpful for premedical advisors and Deans of Admissions to understand that their outcomes will be strengthened if they work in partnership, learning from each other, and appropriately sharing their lessons learned.

*Medical schools should develop clear policies to protect the confidentiality of the admissions process, including the letters of recommendation, while also seeking to support students in their transition to medical school.

*Risks an applicant presents can most often be overcome with openness, honesty, and acceptance of full responsibility for one's actions. This does require evidence of support from those who know the applicant well and are able to speak to their potential for success in medical school and beyond.

*All students should consider the availability of resources a school provides for student wellness and health as a factor in choosing their medical school. This is particularly true for students with any particular risk factors.

QUESTIONS TO GUIDE APPLICANTS

*Are you prepared to discuss with insight and maturity any personal challenges you revealed in your application?

*Do you have the resilience, stress management strategies, and stamina needed to pursue an emotionally and physically demanding career?

*Do you have mentors who are able and willing to write on your behalf in the application process?

*Will you use the resources provided by your school, community, and profession to help you maintain healthy self-care practices throughout your career?

*How can you best use your experiences to guide others as they face similar challenges?

THE CASE OF THE APPLICANT WITH AN EPIPHANY BASED MOTIVATION

BACKGROUND

Many would consider Sarah's upbringing to have been idyllic. Her family had lived and worked on a small farm for several generations with her father's large animal veterinarian practice having its office on the farm as well. Early on, she learned to take responsibility for farm animals and, in helping her father, developed a joy for physical labor and learning about the science she saw come to life on the farm.

Sarah announced at age 10 that she would be a veterinarian herself and set out to achieve this goal. She was a favorite among her teachers throughout her school years because of her enthusiasm for learning, her natural orientation to caring for others combined with her disciplined and mature attitude toward responsibly completing any task assigned. She was also a beloved classmate because of her joy for life and delight in encouraging and supporting others.

An outstanding academic record combined with demonstrated leadership potential and exceptional letters of recommendation from faculty and community leaders led to Sarah's acceptance at several of the strongest pre-vet programs in the country. She chose wisely and entered college with great enthusiasm and focus on her future.

COLLEGE YEARS

Sarah made a smooth transition to all areas of college life. She excelled academically and quickly her peers and administration turned to her for positions of responsibility and leadership. She continued to seek every opportunity to work at the campus internationally ranked vet-hospital and earned several very competitive internships for summer opportunities. She returned home as often as possible and each time, her commitment to one day running her father's practice, was reaffirmed.

During Spring break of her junior year Sarah and her friends traveled to a week-long international movie festival. While watching one of the most popular films, with more than 1,000 in attendance, a horrific mass shooting occurred. In the midst of the chaos, five of Sarah's friends were shot. One died immediately. Sarah began to immediately search for help for her friends and everyone else she encountered. She later would speak with great depth and insight about her emotions as she searched for anyone with EMT equipment. She soon realized she needed to take action. She returned to her friends, made bandages from the clothes they were wearing and, when the shooting returned, worked to cover them with her body and available furniture. When first responders were able to enter the area, Sarah realized the number of casualties would make it impossible for everyone to get the needed treatment in a timely manner. She was able to find a cab driver who entered the building with her, helped her carry her friends to his SUV cab, and took them to the nearest hospital. Sarah shares she will never forget the despair she felt in leaving her deceased friend behind.

Once they arrived at the hospital, Sarah's friends were triaged, with all but one being immediately taken for treatment. As Sarah sat with her friend with less serious injuries, she noticed the needs and panic of the others waiting and began gathering blankets and water for everyone.

When Sarah left the hospital, several days later, having lost another friend to the shooting, she decided this is the work she would do for the rest of her life. She dedicated herself to become a physician and knew she would soon return to a hospital every day of her life.

Sarah returned to College to finish her junior year and shared her new plans with her advisor and family. Everyone was supportive although they all encouraged her to pause and avoid making plans in light of the trauma she had just faced. Sarah was determined to move ahead and immediately made a plan to complete any premedical requirements and to immerse herself in clinical experiences and shadowing opportunities. She applied herself as she always had and within a few months had put together an impressive application for medical school, making clear her focus on becoming an Emergency Medicine physician. She was accepted at four very different programs and chose to attend the program with reportedly the strongest Emergency Medicine residency program.

MEDICAL SCHOOL YEARS

With her maturity and discipline, Sarah easily adjusted to the medical school environment. She immediately sought out relationships in Emergency Medicine and spent every hour available either in the ED or on the research project she had joined which focused on physician post-traumatic stress after mass casualty events. While she excelled in her research, and the Emergency Medicine faculty saw her as extraordinary, she was not as well known by the other faculty. Her Advising Dean helped her see this disparity and she came to understand how it would be a weakness in her preparation. She committed herself to being more fully engaged in each of her classes and clinical teaching opportunities. By the time of graduation, she was applying with a very strong residency application and strong support from her Dean of Students. She was thrilled to match into an outstanding program close to home and found herself surprised to learn how much she looked forward to being able to visit the family home and farm more often.

OUTCOMES

Once again, Sarah took her focus and discipline to her residency training. She excelled and, with the opportunity to spend time every few months back at home, she found herself more relaxed and able to be a role model for her peers in terms of seeking a healthy work-life balance. She was sought after as a mentor for younger residents. She served as Chief Resident and then pursued a fellowship in Disaster Medicine. She felt she had achieved her dreams when she was offered a faculty position in a large city university hospital. She was poised to continue her research, develop her teaching skills, and provide for patients in a Level One trauma center.

After a year in her new position, Sarah felt unsettled and began to ask why she did not have her usual focus on her work. She sought advice from a faculty mentor and in those conversations began to realize that she was very much missing her home, the farm, and the community, now a six-hour drive from her work. Sarah shared that she felt like she was taking her first real breath since the shooting. She began to examine the career and life she had created and began to question if it was the right one. She followed her mentor's advice and resisted making an impulsive decision. She continued to be successful in her faculty role, but also found time to return home regularly. For the first time in years, she had an in-depth conversation with her parents and carefully listened to their feedback.

Sarah continued a careful evaluation of her interests and goals. She began searching for positions closer to home and was pleased to find an opportunity where she could continue to care for patients in an ED and begin to explore her growing interest in teaching disaster response skills to community members.

As Sarah met with her faculty mentor, she thanked her for her patient and wise counsel. Sarah laughingly shared that she would have been a very happy veterinarian, but that she knows she will make important contributions in her work as a physician as long as she stays close to the family and the farm she loves to much. Three years after her return to her local community, Sarah has built a home on the family's land and frequently helps with the farm animals. She is also a regular in attending her father and his new partner in the delivery of large animal patients. She is also a regular speaker at medical schools around the country on disaster response preparedness.

Lessons Learned

*Although moments of great revelation are often powerful and sometimes result in positive personal change, Admissions Committees should proceed with caution to determine that such an epiphany-based motivation will sustain the applicant throughout a career in medicine.

*An applicant's focus on a single career choice during the application process should be carefully explored to insure they will enter medical school with an openness to participate in all areas of the curriculum.

*Applicants should give careful thought and priority to issues of location and availability of support systems as they consider choosing their medical school, residency, and work settings.

Questions to Guide Applicants

*What career choices have you considered during your developmental years? What are the characteristics these have in common?

*Are you making your career decision using strong problem solving strategies, advice from mentors who know you well and an honest self-reflection of your interests and goals.

*If you have experienced significant loss and trauma, have you given yourself the time needed to process this in a healthy manner before making major life decisions?

*Are you entering medical school with an open mind, eager to explore all career path opportunities?

*Are you including consideration of proximity of your support systems as you make choices about your school and work location?

THE CASE OF THE APPLICANT WITH A MISSING DEDICATION TO EXCELLENCE

BACKGROUND

Seemingly everyone loved Marty. At age two, he was regularly described as a "real charmer". As he moved through the elementary school years, his smile and "oh gee" response was celebrated by teachers and peers. He was the first invited to any outing or party. He was also the first chosen when groups were being formed for activities.

His older siblings were the first to express frustration to the adults in Marty's life about the success of his efforts to have others do his chores and homework. His parents chalked this up to his siblings being envious of Marty's natural charm and abilities. Over time however, more and more of Marty's peers began to understand, for example, how any group work with Marty often resulted in others completing his assigned portion. Marty continued to be such a popular and beloved presence with his teachers and all adults in his life that his peers found it easier to just do his work. Marty continued to smile and encourage and thank everyone for their great work.

Marty's college application process proceeded smoothly. His grades and test scores were solid and his letters positive. He did not have significant leadership experiences but was a participant in an impressive breadth of activities. His essays, while demonstrating an inattention to detail, were strong enough. In the end, he has several options and chose a mid-tier small liberal arts college.

COLLEGE YEARS

Without any effort on his part Marty was well known on campus from day one of Orientation. The Admissions Office offered him a job as a campus tour guide and fraternity members were eager to draw him to their houses. He found he was able to achieve solid grades in the general education classes. When his professors asked why he missed classes on a regular basis, he would smile and explain that he really hated not being there to hear their lectures.

The college required their students to choose a major by the beginning of second year and Marty was one of the last students to meet this requirement. When he did eventually meet with his advisor, they decided that he enjoyed sciences and since he was so good with people, he would consider medicine and declared himself to be a premed. Marty continued to achieve solid grades without effort. He was a positive member of his fraternity, but was not interested in the effort and time required to take leadership roles. His peers and faculty soon stopped nominating Marty for positions of responsibility and leadership.

Marty began volunteering weekly at a local hospital and was soon a beloved presence on the floors. He did regularly miss assigned shifts, but his smile and thanks to the volunteer supervisor for understanding, led to no negative consequences. In working with his premedical advisor, he developed a timeline for his medical school application and developed an understanding of what would be necessary for success. He was encouraged when he took an MCAT practice test and determined that with just a few hours of study, he would be able to achieve a score which would be slightly above average.

The medical school application process took more focus and hard work than any effort Marty had previously approached. While his secondary applications were not completed until mid-September and riddled with examples of inattention to detail, he did complete them. With his solid grades and MCAT and letters which stressed his interpersonal gifts and solid academic performance, Marty was invited to interview at three medical schools. He was described as a "star" on interview day and everyone who interviewed him identified him as someone who needed to be accepted, giving him their strongest possible support.

Members of the Admissions Committee found themselves in a robust, sometimes heated discussion when considering Marty's application. At each school, some members advocated for him as a "star" and "a natural in the clinical years". They were passionate in their desire to have him in the class. Others were equally passionate about the errors in his application and the lack of evidence of excellence in any area. He was placed on the waitlist and then the lobbying from individual members began to have him accepted. As a position became available, he was accepted at one large home state school based on enthusiastic support from several prominent faculty members.

MEDICAL SCHOOL YEARS
Marty had never been a focused and dedicated student and therefore found medical school to be the biggest challenge of his life. He simply did not know how to work hard. Initially, he turned to his peers but when he did not prepare for study groups, they were very clear that they could not support his lack of dedication to preparing to be a successful physician. Some of his faculty were initially charmed, but when they saw him approach patient simulations with the same inattention to detail, they became very concerned. He received several negative evaluations and his faculty advisor asked the Dean of Students to help in counseling Marty.

As he began to understand the seriousness of the work he was preparing to do, Marty did begin to focus and apply himself. He became isolated from peers, but gradually, when he did contribute appropriately, they began to reach out and encourage him in his efforts. The third year was difficult in many ways, but Marty worked very hard and was able to pass each of his rotations. In consultation with his faculty advisors, he chose to pursue a residency in Internal Medicine. He prepared these applications with great care and after focused study, he achieved very strong board scores, and was able to match into a program in which he was interested.

OUTCOMES

Marty breathed a sigh of relief at the time of medical school graduation. He felt he had achieved what was needed and had learned that he could work hard and overcome challenges when needed. Unfortunately, he easily returned to his earlier approach to his responsibilities. The nurses regularly described him as a "real charmer" and were initially supportive, overlooking his lack of timely response to their pages. His peers were initially drawn to the positive force of his personality and stepped in to cover the shifts he regularly was unable to take. Although the residency years were not smooth ones, Marty did do enough to finish the program. He joined a private practice and settled into being a mediocre physician who did enough to stay in the group. When asked if, on reflection, he had chosen the right career path, he immediately responded with an emphatic "no". He shared that he thought he would be much more suited to a career in business and was considering taking a leave of absence from the practice so that he could complete an MBA. When he was presented with the option to do an MBA through a nighttime or weekend program, he smiled and shared that he was not interested in working that hard.

LESSONS LEARNED

*Strong applicants will have demonstrated an increasing level of responsibility and leadership in their campus activities.

*Inattention to detail in completing applications should be seen as a potential red flag, perhaps indicating a lack of interest in the application or a lack of commitment to excellence.

*Admissions Committee members views of applicants which diverge sharply should be seen as a caution. This often happens with applicants who bring skills or gifts in one specific area rather than with applicants who bring the breadth of skills and readiness which is important for success in medical school.

*Even when an applicant presents with exceptionally strong interpersonal skills, it is important to explore their motivation for medicine and potential for demonstrating dedication to excellence in their medical school years.

QUESTIONS TO GUIDE APPLICANTS
*How do you know you want a career which requires dedication to working long, often difficult hours?

*What energizes you to give your best sustained effort?

*In what role in a group do you find yourself most comfortable?

*Does your motivation for medicine include a dedication to excellence?

THE CASE OF THE REJECTED APPLICANT WITH "PERFECT NUMBERS"

BACKGROUND

As the only child of parents who were striving to provide him with every needed resource, Steven grew up sharing their focus on success. Early in his education, he was placed in the local public school's Gifted and Talented program where he continued his focus on academic success. From Spelling Bees to Geography Bees to science fairs, Steven was always determined to win and his parents were front and center encouraging his success. Steven's attitude toward competitions gradually changed from a focus on the love of learning and became more focused on defeating other participants. Overtime, this led to fewer and fewer interactions with his peers outside of the classroom or science fair group projects.

Steven and his parents began working with the college counselors early in his high school years. They acted eagerly on the advice received about which AP classes to take and how to prepare for recommended standardized exams. All of their questions centered around the medical school application process in the future.

The advice they received about Steven expanding his involvement with peers and community was confusing to them all. Steven did make some attempts to attend several community service events and club activities. After these attempts, he and his parents concluded this involvement was not worth the investment of his time and he returned to happily focusing his attention in individual pursuits.

The college applications Steven submitted were impressive in terms of the rigor of his curriculum and test scores. Because Steven and his parents were eager for him to attend college close to home, they were pleased when he was accepted to a mid-tier state university nearby.

COLLEGE YEARS

A pattern quickly established of Steven staying in the dorm during the week and going home as early as possible on Friday, returning as late as possible on Sunday. This resulted in Steven not establishing significant relationships with his peers in the living environment.

In meeting with his advisor during the first quarter, Steven learned that an application to medical school would be successful only with evidence of the ability to be a positive team member, a maturity of interpersonal relationships, and dedication to service. Reviewing the experiences of the first-year class of his target medical schools was powerful evidence for what he would need to add to his experiences. In conversation with his parents the following weekend, they decided that Steven's first priority should be becoming involved in a research project. Steven threw his energy into finding a lab and was soon able to find an entry level position.

Steven's image of joining a lab was that he would immediately be involved in all aspects of the project. When his very patient graduate student supervisor laid out the realities of how he would contribute to the lab Steven was disappointed, but determined to do what he had to do to gain medical school admission.

Because he knew medical school was his ultimate goal, Steven decided to apply to several MD programs which accept students at the end of their second year of college. He struggled with the essays that required reflection on his motivation and challenges and was ultimately not accepted. This outcome was disappointing to Steven and his family but the feedback he received about his need to pursue more peer involvement, service activities, and clinical exposure was ignored. As the family talked, they always concluded this advice did not apply in Steven's case because of the strength of his grades and the fact that he was doing everything right.

In regular meetings with his advisor, Steven explained, in response to encouragement to increase his involvement with peers and service, that he simply did not have time in the midst of his academics and research. He turned to the fact that his curriculum was much more rigorous than other students' because of the extent of the AP credit he had used. He also stressed that he had a 4.0 grade point average and knew he would achieve an outstanding MCAT.

As Steven prepared his application to medical school, he again found himself frustrated with many of the questions required. He chose not to complete the questions about challenges he had faced and those about his understanding of health care disparities. He did apply with a 4.0 grade point average and a MCAT score overall in the 99% but did not receive any interview invitations.

During his senior year, Steven did not pay much attention to the rejections he was receiving from schools. He and his parents were so very certain he would be accepted. As graduation neared however, he did begin to take notice and sought advice about what could possibly have gone wrong since he knew he had done everything right. As his advisor again outlined why clinical experience, service orientation and peer relationships are valued in the admissions process Steven remained confused. It was clear in his mind he had done what he needed to do to be a successful applicant to medical school.

MEDICAL SCHOOL YEARS

Steven's parents spoke to many of their friends who recommended that Steven apply to medical schools outside of the United States. And, that in fact, it was not too late to apply for the coming year. A hurried application was submitted and Steven was accepted into an "offshore" medical school.

The transition to the new environment was very difficult for Steven. His parents joined him as much as possible. It was clear from the beginning that he was not well suited for the small group learning required and that he was very uncomfortable in experiences which required patient interaction. At one point, he told his Dean of Students that he found it "very difficult to touch people". For the first time in his life, Steven could not create an academic environment in which he could excel while competing against his peers. He also found himself struggling to take care of his basic needs without his family nearby. Steven did not return to school after the holiday break in his first year of medical school.

When Steven returned home, his parents desperately began searching for ways for him to transfer to a US medical school. As they sought advice from friends, Steven's previous college advisor, and medical school admissions offices they learned this would not be possible.

OUTCOMES

After a few months at home, Steven returned back to his previous lab as a volunteer. He was later hired into an entry level position and worked there for two years as he prepared to apply to PHD programs. He was successful in these applications and has now earned his degree. He has happily returned back to his undergraduate campus and is a research associate in a large, productive lab.

LESSONS LEARNED

*While much of the focus in the admissions process is on the "numbers" required, it is equally important to help applicants understand that excellence in those measures alone will not result in success. Sharing the number of applicants in a cycle who presented with a 4.0 gpa and greater than 96% on the MCAT but were denied without interview, is often helpful for applicants to hear.

*When applicants and their families are unable to hear and trust the advice of well-informed others, they will often turn to those they who understand their perspective, their experiences, and their goals. Premedical advisors and medical school admissions offices in these situations can only listen, work to help the applicant and family find informed advice they do trust, and be available as they hopefully come to trust and accept the evidence presented.

*Even in the absence of a Committee Letter process, it is helpful for undergraduate institutions to develop strategies for premedical students to engage in the self-reflection which will be important for making a well-informed decision for a career in medicine. Evidence of this reflection needs to be a basic requirement in all medical school admissions applications.

*There are many who feel that a sample size of one is sufficient for providing medical school admissions advice. Medical school admissions requirements and policies change over time. Medical schools differ from one another in their missions and commitments. And, differing college backgrounds do impact application success. Unless someone providing advice has continuing experience and insight into all of these factors, their advice, at the very least, should be given little weight in decision making.

QUESTIONS TO GUIDE APPLICANTS

*What have you learned from developing relationships with peers which will allow you to contribute to your medical school community?

*Is service to others a primary piece of your motivation to become a physician?

*Who have you trusted for advice in your medical school application planning? Is there evidence they have the knowledge of current expectations in the admissions process?

*Are you expecting your relative strength in one aspect of your application to overcome your weakness in other areas of expectation?

*Have you engaged in the needed self-reflection to be able to discuss your motivation, strengths, weaknesses, understanding of diversity, resilience, and humility in the application process?

The Case of the Well-Known Applicant

Background

Born to two internationally recognized, high profile parents, Lawrence grew up in a very busy, very loving, and active environment. When their parents were in town, he and his siblings were accustomed to a small part of each day being spent with their parents and the children were also, on many evenings, included in the entertaining of noted visitors. Carefully chosen and supervised staff were an important part of their caregiving as well. From the nanny to the chefs to the security staff, the children felt loved and supported by their version of "family".

Lawrence attended small private schools throughout his elementary and high school years. He was an outstanding student and took advantage of his parents' openness and encouragement for him to be involved in all aspects of a typical high school experience. He excelled in all aspects of the curriculum and found himself most energized by his science classes. He took leadership in science outreach clubs to local elementary school children and was able to do a summer internship in an NIH research program. His parents had a long history of commitment to community service and although their visits to the area soup kitchen and homeless shelter were limited by their schedules to holidays, Lawrence found ways to continue his involvement throughout the school year.

The high school that Lawrence and his siblings attended had extensive experience with high profile families and the challenges this presents in the college application process. The guidance counselors worked closely with the family's tutors and Lawrence to develop his list of schools and the arrangements needed for campus visits. Lawrence's application was outstanding in all areas. His letters of recommendation were particularly noteworthy in the ways in which the faculty spoke to his depth of character and service orientation.

The application process ended with Lawrence having many choices. He and his family chose the school that would provide a strong liberal arts foundation, the opportunity to explore careers in science, including medicine, opportunities for community service, and the campus best prepared to support his security needs. Lawrence himself wrote "thank you notes" to the schools he had visited expressing his appreciation for the opportunities they had arranged for him.

COLLEGE YEARS

Lawrence loved every minute of his college years. He was deeply engaged in his classes, began a research project in his freshman year which he continued to pursue until graduation, and was an active and highly respected leader among his peers in terms of service and campus wellness activities. The only time his classmates and faculty seemed to remember his unusual family situation was on the occasions his parents joined the campus community for events such as Parents' Weekend or graduation.

In the summer after his freshman year, Lawrence participated in a hospital-based internship led by an alum of his college. During this experience, he was able to rotate through many hospital clinical units and at the conclusion, made the decision to pursue a career as a physician. He and his family, in consultation, with his advisors, decided he would apply to medical school at the end of his senior year and take advantage of an opportunity for a fellowship year at the World Health Organization. Lawrence was also gradually taking more of a role in his family's charitable foundation, taking a seat on the Emerging Leaders Board of Directors.

With outstanding grades, a strong MCAT, and extraordinary letters of recommendation, Lawrence submitted his AMCAS application in June and had completed all of his secondaries by August. He had developed his school list in close consultation with his advisor and security team, focusing on schools that his advisor had been assured by the medical school deans would be able to accommodate his unique needs during an interview day visit.

Lawrence was invited to interview at six schools. His interview day proceeded smoothly at the first two medical schools. The admissions offices and security leadership had successfully maintained confidentially of the news of his visit. The faculty and students chosen to participate in interviewing Lawrence were privately briefed and he was able to participate in all aspects of the interview day.

When Lawrence visited a third school for interview, his security detail expressed grave concerns when the protestors in front of the medical school building made it clear on the interview day morning that the news of Lawrence's presence on campus was widely known. Their concern was so great that the decision was made for Lawrence to leave the campus before interviews began and withdraw his application to the remaining three schools. His security staff felt this was very necessary even knowing that he would perhaps need to reapply if unsuccessful in the two interview days he had been able to attend.

The admissions committee deliberations at both schools raised a number of concerns. Several members felt this was an applicant of great privilege who would, because of his wealth, never practice medicine. Other members asked if accepting Lawrence would mean four or more years of constant security concerns which the school would be needing to address and fund. The debates were spirited, but in the end, Lawrence's outstanding overall application led the committee to accept him based on his own merits. The majority of committee members felt he had provided strong evidence for his motivation and commitment to medicine.

After receiving an acceptance to the two schools where he was able to interview, Lawrence chose his school based on consultation with his advisors, parents, and security staff. He was also pleased to learn that two of his friends from college would be attending the same program, feeling they could be a help in his efforts to integrate into the medical school as "just another student".

Lawrence was anything but "just another student" during his medical school years. The clarity of his motivation, his sincere gratitude for the opportunity to study to be a physician, and his exceptional maturity and interpersonal skills made him a stand-out "star" in the classroom and in the clinics. The only time the high-profile status of his family became an issue was when the time came to choose graduation speakers. On behalf of the Dean of Students Office, Lawrence was able to reach out to a well-known family friend who was eager to participate.

With his presence on the Emerging Leaders board of his family foundation, the group began to add a focus on issues of public health and health care disparities. After careful discussion with his faculty mentors, he decided to take a leave of absence from medical school after his third year to pursue a Master's in Health Policy and was feeling more and more that he wanted the Foundation to remain an aspect of his future career. During his Master's year, Lawrence was able to travel for the Foundation and expand the network of the Foundation's partner organizations. At the end of the year, he was very much looking forward to returning to the clinics for his fourth year and had decided to ultimately pursue a specialty in Infectious Diseases.

OUTCOMES

After a very successful residency and fellowship Lawrence was enthusiastic to move into his role as a junior faculty member within an academic medical center. Lawrence was grateful to have the opportunity for this position in an institution with a long history of supporting faculty in their philanthropic commitments. His work with his family's foundation had given him opportunities to lead important research projects in Infectious Diseases. And, his personal joy in serving as a mentor and teacher continued to energize his teaching. Lawrence regularly shared, however, that he found his true passion in his clinical work. Even as his promotions made clinical time less and less expected, Lawrence continued his commitment to seeing patients. He is a beloved colleague and mentor, regularly winning awards given by students and is a member of the institution's Academy of Distinguished Educators. His work with his family's foundation continues and his son and daughter are both now important voices on the Emerging Leaders Board of Directors.

LESSONS LEARNED
*Medical School Admissions offices must be committed to the highest standards of maintaining confidentiality in all aspects of the

admissions process. The practices and strategies required to meet the needs of best practice must be carefully and regularly reviewed.

*Medical schools should prioritize developing and maintaining strong relationships with their campus security partners. The benefits of this will be seen in addressing a number of potential problems but certainly when arrangements are being made for high profile individuals to attend events on campus.

*Individuals from backgrounds of great privilege should be evaluated on their individual achievement, character, potential, and goals. Great privilege alone is not a disqualifying factor. Admissions committee members are encouraged to consider their potential biases when evaluating these candidates.

QUESTIONS TO GUIDE APPLICANTS
*How will you use the many privileges you have been given to make a difference through your career in medicine?

*Given the challenges of your particular circumstances, will you be able to focus on the demands of medical school.

*Why is becoming a physician the best way for you to use your abilities   and   interests?

THE CASE OF THE APPLICANT WITH A LONG DISTANCE TRAVELED

BACKGROUND

Growing up in a multicultural family with a tradition of incorporating traditions from their diverse backgrounds, Kerry's family was rich in pride for their heritage and joy in their intergenerational home. They were not rich, however, in terms of economic resources nor educational opportunities. Kerry and her five siblings and four cousins lived in the same house where it was easy to find wonderful aromas coming out of the kitchen, but difficult to find a quiet space to study. Nevertheless, Kerry was able to graduate from high school with a strong academic record and experience in working multiple jobs to help contribute to her family's needs. Her parents and aunts and uncles did not encourage Kerry's interest in attending college and it was clear that their expectation was for her to finish high school and begin a full-time job.

Her high school biology teacher had come to know Kerry during her freshman year when Kerry had served as an English as a Second Language Aide for a new Special Needs student. She had encouraged Kerry to consider continued education after high school and year by year, Kerry began to see that as a possibility. The biology teacher sought the support of a guidance counselor and between the two of them and a small school grant, they were able to help Kerry gain acceptance to a four-year university close to home. Kerry was thrilled. Her family agreed she could attend college for one-year as long as she continued to live at home and help with expenses.

COLLEGE YEARS

Kerry's high school teacher and counselor gave her very good advice about how to prepare for the transition to college and what do expect. This was very important as Kerry faced many challenges which ranged from not being able to afford required materials, to the need to work 20-hours/week while also commuting from home, and the family expectations that she would continue to participate in weekly family gatherings. Kerry maintained a very positive and eager attitude in the midst of these demands. She had expected the hurdles and absolutely loved and was energized by her classes.

At the end of her first year, her family agreed she could stay in college as long as she continued to meet all of her responsibilities. The demands she faced did impact her grades, but given her realities, they were still impressive. She was on track to graduate with a B.S. in Neurobiology and a minor in Psychology. Her science and non-science gpa averages were both 3.4.

Because of her interest in science and her experience as a caregiver for her family and in an area nursing home, at the end of her second year, Kerry made an appointment to meet with the campus pre-medical advisor. The advising office was very busy, so the appointment was long awaited. The 15-minute appointment however was very distressing for Kerry. The information the advisor shared was accurate and she did learn the timeline for an application to medical school. She also left with material to explore alternate health care careers. In her conversation with her high school mentors which followed, Kerry shared that she was told she would not be able to get into medical school with her grades so she would have to consider other options. Her high school mentors were confused, but since they knew they were not qualified to give advice about medical school applications, they continued to encourage her to focus on graduation. With their direction, Kerry did seek advice on how she could achieve teaching certification so that she could become a high school biology teacher.

Kerry quickly became a beloved and respected teacher who served as an inspiration to the many students who gathered around her desk for advice at any possible moment. As her fellow science teachers came to know her and learn about her family, one of the teachers asked to speak to Kerry privately. He explained that his wife was a physician and would be happy to talk with her about medical school possibilities. Kerry could only remember her feeling after the meeting with the college premedical advisor and did not want to be embarrassed in front of her colleague's spouse. She initially politely turned down the offer, but over time, did agree to have coffee with the colleague and his wife.

The meeting was transformative for Kerry. The physician shared stories of several of her colleagues with backgrounds similar to Kerry's. She shared the name of a premedical advisor who had previously been open to helping some applicants in Kerry's situation. Within weeks, Kerry had met with the advisor, learned of the steps she would need to take, achieved an average score on a MCAT practice exam, and had renewed hope that maybe she could become a doctor. The advisor continued to encourage Kerry and at the end of the next application cycle, Kerry had acceptance to two medical schools. She received significant need based financial aid from both schools, and with the advisor's help, made the choice to attend the school with the strongest Office of Multicultural Affairs programming and resources.

Kerry's family did not approve when she shared this news. More years of schooling did not make sense in their experience. Kerry's determination was clear, however. When she chose a school that was five hours away from home, there were more concerns expressed, but Kerry did not waver in her goals.

MEDICAL SCHOOL YEARS

The Dean for Multicultural Affairs was eager to welcome Kerry to medical school. During orientation events, there were events for Kerry to meet with other students who had also traveled paths that were more challenging than most medical school matriculants. This group quickly became a source of great support and encouragement for Kerry. Given her new confidence in her ability to succeed and belong in medical school, Kerry also became involved with many community service groups and developed a special interest in, and eventually took leadership in, a local free clinic focused on the needs of a community much like the one in which she had been raised.

The Director of Financial Aid was also an important resource for Kerry as she learned to manage the complexities of the student budget. While her instinct was to continue to send money home to help her family's expenses, the Director of Financial Aid was very helpful in outlining the trade-off between contributing to her family now and accruing additional debt.

Kerry excelled in all aspects of medical school. She was an encouraging mentor for those the Multicultural Affairs Office asked her to advise during the admissions process and through the matriculation transition. She decided to pursue a career in Family Medicine and was eagerly accepted in her top choice residency.

OUTCOMES

After completing her residency Kerry was recruited by several practice groups. She chose the position that allowed her to be closer to her family. In discussing her goals during the recruiting process, she made it clear she wanted to have the flexibility to devote a portion of her time to doing outreach programs for the local high school and colleges so that she could encourage students to see their possibilities in a career in medicine.

LESSONS LEARNED

*Premedical students are vulnerable to the advice they receive from their peers, faculty, and premedical advisors. This is particularly true of students who come from nontraditional premedical backgrounds. The professional staff with responsibility for advising premedical applicants, must see the possibilities in their applicants. Rather than stating that their goal is likely impossible, it is important to in an encouraging manner, state the steps that would be needed for success.

*Admissions Committees cannot "guess" an applicant will be successful, but they can take into account the level of success achieved by an applicant in the midst of unusual challenges faced. Analysis of prior student performance can give insight into the profiles required to thrive in their individual school's curriculum.

*Offices of Multicultural Affairs must develop strategies for students who have traveled unusual distances to see themselves and their potential for success in their peers and faculty.

*The Office of Financial Aid can be an important partner in an Admissions Committee's efforts to help students from non-traditional backgrounds be able to make a successful transition to medical school.

QUESTIONS TO GUIDE APPLICANTS

*Have you found knowledgeable advisors and mentors who respect your experiences and encourage and support you in your journey to medicine?

*Can you identify and develop strategies to meet the challenges you will face, and the sacrifices required to achieve your goals in medicine?

*Are you prepared to use the resources of your school Financial Aid office to make informed choices about funding your medical school education?

*How will you use your experiences to encourage others throughout your career?

SUMMARY OF LESSONS LEARNED

Below you will find the **Lessons Learned** which have been included at the end of each case study.

ACADEMIC READINESS

*A passion for learning across disciplines, with a particular interest in the sciences is required as a part of an appropriate motivation for, and success in, a career in medicine.

*Experience with a combination of rigorous science classes at one time is important in evaluating potential for success in the medical school curriculum.

ADMISSIONS COMMITTEE RESPONSIBILITIES

*While family, supporters, development officers, and schools may think they are being helpful in paving the way for admission for applicants, this seldom leads to a positive outcome. The best processes have firewalls to prevent this influence from impacting admissions decisions.

*It is important that the medical school interview process allow for the identification of the quiet and steady leaders who are often overlooked in the face of more extroverted applicants.

*College faculty, premedical advisors and admissions committees should examine the biases they hold regarding issues of religion and the practice of medicine.

*It is important to respect the journeys and diverse perspective and experiences of applicants who are first generation college students.

*Applicants enter the medical school application process with a great variance in terms of their maturity and readiness. Admissions Committees should be aware that in some cases, substantial help may have been provided.

*There are often signs during the admissions process that suggest an applicant's parents are overly involved. In these situations, the applicant's maturity, independence, and readiness should be given additional evaluation.

*In reviewing who has submitted letters of recommendation on behalf of the applicant, it is important to consider those that are submitted, as well as, those that are not chosen for submission.

*Tragedy and hardship can lead to the resilience and determination needed for success as a medical school student and physician. It should not, however, be seen as a reason to overlook or explain away any aspect of the applicant's record.

*It is very helpful for premedical advisors and Dean of Admissions to understand that their outcomes will be strengthened if they work in partnership, learning from each other, and appropriately sharing their lessons learned.

*Medical schools should develop clear policies to protect the confidentiality of the admissions process, including the letters of recommendation, while also seeking to support students in their transition to medical school.

*Admissions Committee members views of applicants which diverge sharply should be seen as a caution. This often happens with applicants who bring skills or gifts in one specific area rather than with applicants who bring the breadth of skills and readiness which is important for success in medical school.

*Medical School Admissions offices must be committed to the highest standards of maintaining confidentiality in all aspects of the admissions process. The practices and strategies required to meet the needs of best practice must be carefully and regularly reviewed.

*Medical schools should prioritize developing and maintaining strong relationships with their campus security partners. The benefits of this will be seen in a number of potential problems, but certainly when arrangements are being made for high profile individuals to attend events on campus.

*Individuals from backgrounds of great privilege should be evaluated on their individual achievement, character, potential, and goals. Great privilege alone is not a disqualifying factor. Admissions committee members are encouraged to consider their potential biases when evaluating these candidates.

*Admissions committees can be blinded by extraordinary extracurricular leadership and interpersonal skills. Don't be.

*Admissions Committees cannot "guess" an applicant will be successful, but they can take into account the level of success achieved by an applicant in the midst of the unusual challenges faced. Analysis of prior student success can give insight into the profiles required to thrive in their individual school's curriculum.

*Offices of Multicultural Affairs must develop strategies for students who have traveled unusual distances to see themselves and their potential for success in their peers and faculty.

*The Office of Financial Aid can be an important partner in an Admissions Committee's efforts to help students from non-traditional backgrounds be able to make a successful transition to medical school.

ADVISOR CHALLENGES AND RESPONSIBILITIES

*Applicants will hear advice from those who are ill informed about current standards for medical school admissions perspectives. It is important to give them opportunities to hear the correct advice from resources that can supplement the advisor's advice.

*Advisors face very complicated demands and sometimes competing roles. Their constituents include the applicant, the applicant's parents, the institution's enrollment goals, the faculty who support the premedical curriculum, the medical schools, and the applicant's future patients. It is important they receive full support for their work from their institutions.

*It is very helpful for college faculty to make themselves available for interviews with applicants, using the personal statement and activities as material for their questions.

*It is important to respect the journeys and diverse perspective and experiences of applicants who are first generation college students.

*College faculty, premedical advisors and admissions committees should examine the biases they hold regarding issues of religion and the practice of medicine.

*Risks an applicant presents can most often be overcome with openness, honesty, and acceptance of full responsibility for one's actions. This does require evidence of support from those who know the applicant well and are able to speak to their potential for success in medical school and beyond.

*While much of the focus in the admissions process is on the "numbers" required it is equally important to help applicants understand that excellence in those measures alone will not result in success. Sharing the number of applicants in a cycle who presented with a 4.0 gpa and greater than 96% on the MCAT, but were denied without interview is helpful for applicants to hear.

*When applicants and their families are unable to hear and trust the advice of well-informed others, they will often turn to those they know who understand their perspective, their experiences, and their goals. Premedical advisors and medical school admissions offices in these situations can only listen, work to help the applicant and family find informed advice they do trust and be available as they hopefully come to eventually trust and accept the evidence presented.

*Even in the absence of a Committee Letter process it is helpful for undergraduate institutions to develop strategies for premedical students to engage in the self-reflection which will be important for making a well-informed decision for a career in medicine. Evidence of this reflection needs to be a basic requirement in all medical school admissions applications.

*There are many who feel that a sample size of one is sufficient for providing medical school advice. Medical school admissions requirements and policies change over time. Medical schools differ from one another in their missions and commitments. And, differing college backgrounds do impact application success. Unless someone providing advice has continuing experience and insight into all of these factors, their advice, at the very least, should be given little weight in decision making.

*Premedical students are vulnerable to the advice they receive from their peers, faculty and premedical advisors. This is particularly true of students who come from nontraditional premedical backgrounds. The professional staff with responsibility for advising premedical applicants, must see the possibilities in their applicants. Rather than stating that their goal is likely impossible, it is important to, in an encouraging manner, state the steps that would be needed for success.

CULTURAL COMPETENCE
*In discussing the role of faith in one's motivation for medicine, it is important to make clear a dedication to respect and celebrate the religious beliefs and traditions of all others.

ISSUES OF MOTIVATION
*Decisions made to become a physician early in life must be reexamined carefully with mature reflection on how interests and strengths have developed.

*Applicants will find the best fit in their medical school search by identifying their priorities and the strength of the resources available on each campus to pursue these.

*The decision to decline a medical school acceptance offer with hopes to reapply and gain an offer at a school perceived as stronger should be seen as a major concern in terms of the applicant's motivation and priorities.

*Although moments of great revelation are often powerful and sometimes result in positive personal change, Admissions Committees should proceed with caution to determine that such an epiphany-based motivation will sustain the applicant throughout a career in medicine.

*An applicant's focus on a single career choice during the application process should be carefully explored to insure they will enter medical school with an openness to participate in all areas of the curriculum.

*Inattention to detail in completing applications should be seen as a potential red flag, perhaps indicating a lack of interest in the application or a lack of commitment to excellence.

*Even when an applicant presents with exceptionally strong interpersonal skills, it is important to explore their motivation for medicine and potential for demonstrating dedication to excellence in their medical school years.

PERSONAL READINESS
*Institutional actions should not be disqualifying, but evidence is required to demonstrate the needed level of responsibility, maturity, and integrity.

*Strong letters of recommendation from those who know the applicant well are always important, but particularly so in cases where institutional actions are an issue.

RESILIENCE AND ADAPTABILITY
*Evidence of resilience is required to suggest readiness for medical school.

*Evidence of the strategies needed for making successful transitions are important to consider in the medical school admissions process.

*All students should consider the availability of resources a school provides for student wellness and health as a factor in choosing their medical school. This is particularly true for students with any particular risk factors.

*Applicants should give careful thought and priority to issues of location and availability of support systems as they consider choosing their medical school.

SERVICE ORIENTATION

*A history of, enthusiasm for, sustained participation in service, and clinical activities are important in predicting success in medical school.

INTERPERSONAL READINESS
*Strong applicants will have demonstrated an increasing level of responsibility and leadership in their campus activities.

SUMMARY OF QUESTIONS TO GUIDE APPLICANTS

Below you will find the **Questions To Guide Applicants** provided at the end of each case study.

ACADEMIC READINESS

*Are you energized by your science classes and find yourself able to excel in those academic terms when you take more than one science class?

*Will you be eager to be a life-long learner, particularly in the sciences?

ISSUES OF MOTIVATION

*If you made your decision to become a physician at a young age, have you honestly reexamined your motivation as you have matured?

*Are you passionate about using your life in service to others, putting the needs of others before your own?

*If you could anything you could dream of in the coming year what would it be? Does it embody the values of learning and service?

*What resources are important to you as you live a life which is true to the values which shape and sustain you?

*Why is a career as a physician the best way for you to achieve your life's goals?

*How is your decision to pursue medicine influenced and directed by family expectations?

*Does your decision to become a physician see prestige as a primary motivation?

*How can you best use your experiences to guide others as they face similar challenges?

*What career choices have you considered during your developmental years? What are the characteristics these have in common?

*Are you making your career decision using strong problem solving strategies, advice from mentors who know you well and an honest self-reflection of your interests and goals.

*Are you entering medical school with an open mind, eager to explore all career path opportunities?

*How do you know you want a career which requires dedication to working long, often difficult hours?

*What energizes you to give your best sustained effort?

*Does your motivation for medicine include a dedication to excellence?

*Is service to others a primary piece of your motivation to become a physician?

*How will you use the many privileges you have been given to make a difference through your career in medicine?

*Why is becoming a physician the best way for you to use your abilities and interests?

*How will you use your experiences to encourage others throughout your career?

APPLICATION PLANNING

*There is no one right path to college and medical school. Find the path right for you and begin college or medical school only when you are ready to excel in all areas of your life. Sometimes this will require taking time in between graduation and matriculation. What can you do during this time to strengthen your readiness?

*Are you able to obtain letters of recommendation which speak to your maturity, integrity, motivation and intellectual and personal readiness to be an outstanding medical student?

*Do you respect the experience and advice of others?

*Are you ready to complete the application to medical school without significant guidance, input, and contribution from your parents?

*Have you sought advice about your career interests from trusted mentors, in several areas of your life, who have come to know you well?

*Are you able to identify and accept feedback from appropriate and knowledgeable resources to guide you in your professional decision making?

*Do you have mentors who are able and willing to write on your behalf in the application process?

*Are you including consideration of proximity of your support systems as you make choices about your school and work location?

*Who have you trusted for advice in your medical school application planning? Is there evidence they have the knowledge of current expectations in the admissions process?

*Are you expecting your relative strength in one aspect of your application to overcome your weakness in other areas of expectation?

*Have you found knowledgeable advisors and mentors who respect your experiences and encourage and support you in your journey to medicine?

*Are you prepared to use the resources of your school Financial Aid office to make informed choices about funding your medical school education?

RESILIENCE AND ADAPTABILITY
*Have you learned how to "bounce" back, to do something that requires hard work and persistence. Have you developed resilience?

*Have you learned to accept less than perfection from yourself in some of your efforts? Are you able to contribute in situations where you are not the "star"?

*If you had a difficult transition to college, what have you learned that insures your transition to medical will be successful?

*How will you develop a support system in medical school that allows you to learn with and from those with similar values and goals?

*Are you prepared to discuss with insight and maturity any personal challenges you revealed in your application?

*Do you have the resilience, stress management strategies, and stamina needed to pursue an emotionally and physically demanding career?

*Will you use the resources provided by your school, community, and profession to help you maintain healthy self-care practices throughout your career?

*If you have experienced significant loss and trauma, have you given yourself the time needed to process this in a healthy manner before making major life decisions?

*Given the challenges of your particular circumstances, will you be able to focus on the demands of medical school.

*Can you identify and develop strategies to meet the challenges you will face, and the sacrifices required to achieve your goals in medicine?

INTERPERSONAL READINESS
*Are you eager to work together with a team to achieve a common goal?

*In what role in a group do you find yourself most comfortable?

*Have you learned to live as an independent adult, taking care of your needs in all areas of your life while also supporting those around you?

*Are you dedicated to growing as a culturally competent person and future physician?

*What have you learned from developing relationships with peers which will allow you to contribute to your medical school community?

ACKNOWLEDGMENTS

The support of many is what made it possible for me to complete this project. Thank you to Gary, Alyson, Jim, Charles, and Jamie who read the initial cases and encouraged me to continue. Thank you to Lidia Waltos for her patient review and feedback.

Thank you to my admissions mentors. To Norma Wagoner, Janis Mendelsohn, Eric Lombard, Ed Dodson, Gab Garcia, Al Kirby, Judy Colwell, Anthony Montag, and Brenda Armstrong. They all taught me what it means to do a holistic review before the term was coined.

Thank you to Jamie Marion for always making my ideas better. It was her insight that led me to add the sections on questions for applicants. I know her input has made this a more useful tool.

Thank you to the faculty members who dedicated their time and shared their wisdom to do the work of the Admissions Committee during my years at the University of Chicago. I am very grateful for the privilege of learning from their lives dedicated to service and life-learning.

Thank you to the tens of thousands who have allowed me to read their applications, to the thousands I have interviewed, and the hundreds I have helped choose the right medical school. And, finally, thank you to those I continue to advise. I am honored to be part of your journey as each of you seeks to live a life dedicated to service and life-long learning.

Made in the USA
Las Vegas, NV
14 March 2024

87218462R00049